SHALL WE KNOW ONE ANOTHER?

&

OTHER PAPERS

J.C. RYLE

CHARLES NOLAN PUBLISHERS
MOSCOW

First published by Cassell, Petter, & Galpin [1870?]
First Charles Nolan Publishers edition 2001
 Published 2001
Printed in the United States of America
This book is printed on acid-free paper.
ISBN 0-9677603-6-4

CHARLES NOLAN PUBLISHERS
MOSCOW, IDAHO
UNITED STATES OF AMERICA

CONTENTS

SHALL WE KNOW ONE ANOTHER? 1

I PITY that man who never thinks about heaven. I use that word in the broadest and most popular sense. I mean by "heaven" the future dwelling-place of all true Christians, when the dead are raised, and the world has passed away. Cold and unfeeling must that heart be which never gives a thought to that dwelling place! Dull and earthly must that mind be which never considers "heaven"!

We may die any day. "In the midst of life we are in death."[1] We must all die sooner or later. The youngest, the fairest, the strongest, the cleverest, all must go down one day before the scythe of the King of Terrors. This world shall not go on forever as it does now. Its affairs shall at last be wound up. The King of kings will come, and take His great power, and reign. The judgment shall be set, the books opened, the dead raised, the living changed. And where do we all hope to go then? Why, if we know anything of true faith in the Lord Jesus Christ, we hope to go to "heaven." Surely there is nothing unreasonable in asking men to consider the subject of heaven.

Now what will heaven be like? The question, no doubt, is a deep one, but there is nothing presumptuous in looking at it. The man who is about to sail for Australia or New Zealand as a settler is naturally anxious to know something about his future home, its climate, its employments, its inhabitants, its ways, its customs. All these are subjects of deep interest to him. You are leaving the land of your nativity; you are going to spend the rest of your life in a new hemisphere. It would be strange indeed if you did not desire information about your new abode. Now surely, if we hope to dwell forever in that

[1] Book of Common Prayer.

"better country, even an heavenly one,"[1] we ought to seek all the knowledge we can get about it. Before we go to our eternal home, we should try to become acquainted with it.

There are many things about heaven revealed in Scripture which I purposely pass over. That it is a prepared place for a prepared people; that all who are found there will be of one mind and of one experience, chosen by the same Father, washed in the same blood of atonement, renewed by the same Spirit; that universal and perfect holiness, love, and knowledge will be the eternal law of the kingdom—all these are ancient things, and I do not mean to dwell on them. Suffice it to say that heaven is the eternal presence of everything that can make a saint happy, and the eternal absence of everything that can cause sorrow. Sickness, and pain, and disease, and death, and poverty, and labour, and money, and care, and ignorance, and misunderstanding, and slander, and lying, and strife, and contention, and quarrels, and envies, and jealousies, and bad tempers, and infidelity, and scepticism, and irreligion, and superstition, and heresy, and schism, and wars, and fightings, and bloodshed, and murders, and lawsuits—all, all these things shall have no place in heaven. On earth, in this present time, they may live and flourish. In heaven even their footprints shall not be known.

Hear what the inspired apostle St. John says:

> There shall in no wise enter into it anything that defileth, neither whatsoever worketh abomination, or maketh a lie: but they which are written in the Lamb's book of life. (Rev. 21:27)
>
> There shall be no night there; and they need no candle, neither light of the sun; for the Lord God giveth them light: and they shall reign for ever and ever. (Rev. 22:5)
>
> They shall hunger no more, neither thirst any more; neither shall the sun light on them, nor any heat. For the Lamb which is in the midst of the throne shall feed them, and shall lead them unto living fountains of waters: and God shall wipe away all tears from their eyes. (Rev. 7:16, 17)

[1] Heb. 11:16.

> There shall be no more death, neither sorrow, nor crying, neither shall there be any more pain: for the former things are passed away. (Rev. 21:4)

Hear what that glorious dreamer, John Bunyan, says, though writing with an uninspired pen:

> I saw in my dream that these two men, Christian and Hopeful, went in at the gate. And lo! as they entered, they were transfigured, and they had raiment put on that shone like gold. There were also that met them with harps and crowns, and gave them to them; the harps to praise withal, and the crowns in token of honour. Then I heard in my dream that all the bells in the city rang again for joy, and that it was said unto them, "Enter ye into the joy of our Lord."[1] I also heard the men themselves sing with a loud voice, saying, "Blessing, and honour, and glory, and power, be unto Him that sitteth upon the throne, and unto the Lamb for ever and ever."[2]
>
> Now, just as the gates were opened to let in the men, I looked in after them, and behold the city shone like the sun; the streets also were paved with gold, and in them walked many men with crowns on their heads, palms in their hands, and golden harps to sing praises withal.
>
> There were also of them that had wings, and they answered one another without intermission, saying, "Holy, holy, holy, is the Lord."[3] And after that they shut up the gates; which, when I had seen, I wished myself among them.[4]

But I will not dwell on these things. I purposely pass by them all. I wish to confine myself in this paper to one single point of deep and momentous interest. That point is the mutual recognition of saints in the next world. I want to examine the question, "Shall we know one another in heaven?"

Now what saith the Scripture on this subject? This is the only thing I care to know. I grant freely that there are not many texts in the Bible which touch the subject at all. I admit fully that pious and learned divines are not of one mind with

[1] Matt. 25:21. [2] Rev. 5:13. [3] Isa. 6:3.
[4] John Bunyan (1628–1688), *Pilgrim's Progress*.

me about the matter in hand. I have listened to many ingenious reasonings and arguments against the view that I maintain. But in theology I dare not call any man master and father. My only aim and desire is to find out what the Bible says, and to take my stand upon its teaching.

Let us hear what David said when his child was dead. "Now he is dead, wherefore should I fast? can I bring him back again? I shall go to him, but he shall not return to me." (2 Sam. 12:23.) What can these words mean, but that David hoped to see his child, and meet him again, in another world? This was evidently the hope that cheered him, and made him dry his tears. The separation would not be forever.

Let us hear what St. Paul said to the Thessalonians. "What is our hope, or joy, or crown of rejoicing? Are not even ye in the presence of our Lord Jesus Christ at His coming?" (1 Thess. 2:19.) These words must surely mean that the apostle expected to recognise his beloved Thessalonian converts in the day of Christ's second advent. He rejoiced in the thought that he would see them face to face at the last day; would stand side by side with them before the throne, and would be able to say, "Here am I, and the seals which thou didst give to my ministry."

Let us hear what the same apostle says, in the same epistle, for the comfort of mourners. "I would not have you to be ignorant, brethren, concerning them which are asleep, that ye sorrow not, even as others which have no hope. For if we believe that Jesus died and rose again, even so them also which sleep in Jesus will God bring with Him." (1 Thess. 4:13, 14.) There would be no point in these words of consolation if they did not imply the mutual recognition of saints. The hope with which he cheers wearied Christians is the hope of meeting their beloved friends again. He does not merely say, "Sorrow not, for they are at rest—they are happy—they are free from pain and trouble—they are better off than they would be here below." No! he goes a step further. He says, "God shall bring them with Christ, when He brings them back to the world. You are not parted forever. You will meet again."

I commend these three passages to the reader's attentive consideration. To my eye, they all seem to point to only one conclusion. They all imply the same great truth that saints in heaven shall know one another. They shall have the same body and the same character that they had on earth—a body perfected and transformed like Christ's in His transfiguration, but still the same body—a character perfected and purified from all sin, but still the same character. But in the moment that we who are saved shall meet our several friends in heaven, we shall at once know them, and they will at once know us.

There is something to my mind unspeakably glorious in this prospect: few things so strike me in looking forward to the good things yet to come. Heaven will be no strange place to us when we get there. We shall not be oppressed by the cold, shy, chilly feeling that we know nothing of our companions. We shall feel at home. We shall see all of whom we have read in Scripture, and know them all, and mark the peculiar graces of each one. We shall look upon Noah, and remember his witness for God in ungodly times. We shall look on Abraham, and remember his faith; on Isaac, and remember his meekness; on Moses, and remember his patience; on David, and remember all his troubles. We shall sit down with Peter, and James, and John, and Paul, and remember all their toil when they laid the foundations of the Church. Blessed and glorious will that knowledge and communion be! If it is pleasant to know one or two saints, and meet them occasionally now, what will it be to know them all, and to dwell with them forever!

There is something unspeakably comforting, moreover, as well as glorious in this prospect. It lights up the valley of the shadow of death. It strips the sick bed and the grave of half their terrors. Our beloved friends who have fallen asleep in Christ are not lost, but only gone before. The children of the same God and partakers of the same grace can never be separated very long. They are sure to come together again when this world has passed away. Our pleasant communion with our kind Christian friends is only broken off for a small moment, and is soon to be eternally resumed. These eyes of ours shall once more look upon their faces, and these ears of ours shall once more hear them speak. Blessed and happy indeed will that meeting be!—better a thousand times than the parting! We parted in sorrow, and we shall meet in joy; we parted in stormy weather, and we shall meet in a calm harbour; we parted amidst pains and aches, and groans, and infirmities: we shall meet with glorious bodies, able to serve our Lord forever without distraction. And, best of all, we shall meet never to be parted, never to shed one more tear, never to put on mourning, never to say goodbye and farewell again. Oh! it is a blessed thought that saints will know one another in heaven!

How much there will be to talk about! What wondrous wisdom will appear in everything that we had to go through in the days of our flesh! We shall remember all the way by which we were led, and say, "Wisdom and mercy followed me all the days of my life. In my sicknesses and pains, in my losses and crosses, in my poverty and tribulations, in my bereavements and separation, in every bitter cup I had to drink, in every burden I had to carry, in all these was perfect wisdom." We shall see it at last, if we never saw it before, and we shall all see it together, and all unite in praising Him that "led us by the right way to a city of habitation."[1] Surely, next to the thought of seeing Christ in heaven, there is no more blessed and happy thought than that of seeing one another.

Shall we get to heaven at all? This, after all, is the grand question which the subject should force on our attention, and which we should resolve, like men, to look in the face. What shall it profit you and me to study theories about a future

[1] Ps. 107:7.

state, if we know not on which side we shall be found at the last day? Let us arouse our sleepy minds to a consideration of this momentous question. Heaven, we must always remember, is not a place where all sorts and kinds of persons will go as a matter of course. The inhabitants of heaven are not such a discordant, heterogeneous rabble as some men seem to suppose. Heaven, it cannot be too often remembered, is a prepared place for a prepared people. The dwellers in heaven will be all of one heart and one mind, one faith and one character. They will be ready for mutual recognition. But, are we ready for it? are we in tune? Shall we ourselves get to heaven?

Why should we not get to heaven? Let us set that question also before us, and fairly look it in the face. There sits at the right hand of God One who is able to save to the uttermost all them that come unto God by Him, and One who is as willing to save as He is able. The Lord Jesus Christ has died for us on the cross, and paid our mighty debt with His own blood. He is sitting at God's right hand, to be the Advocate and Friend of all who desire to be saved. He is waiting at this moment to be gracious. Surely, if we do not get to heaven the fault will be all our own. Let us arise and lay hold on the hand that is held out to us from heaven. Let us never forget that promise, "If we confess our sins, He is faithful and just to forgive us our sins, and to cleanse us from all unrighteousness." (1 John 1:9.) The prison doors are set wide open; let us go forth and be free. The lifeboat is alongside; let us embark in it and be safe. The bread of life is before us; let us eat and live. The Physician stands before us; let us hear His voice, believe, and make sure our interest in heaven.

Have we a good hope of going to heaven, a hope that is scriptural, reasonable, and will bear investigation? Then let us not be afraid to meditate often on the subject of "heaven," and to rejoice in the prospect of good things to come. I know that even a believer's heart will sometimes fail when he thinks of the last enemy and the unseen world. Jordan is a cold river to cross at the very best, and not a few tremble when they think of their own crossing. But let us take comfort in the remembrance of the other side. Think, Christian reader, of seeing your Saviour, and beholding your King in His beauty. Faith will be at last swallowed up in sight and hope in certainty. Think of the many loved ones gone before you, and of the happy meeting between you and them. You are not going to a foreign country; you are going home. You are not going to dwell amongst strangers, but amongst friends. You will find them all safe, all well, all ready to greet you, all prepared to join in one unbroken song of praise. Then let us take comfort and persevere. With such prospects before us, we may well cry, "It is worthwhile to be a Christian!"

I conclude all with a passage from *Pilgrim's Progress*, which well deserves reading.

> Said Pliable to Christian, "What company shall we have in heaven?"
>
> Christian replied, "There we shall be with seraphim and cherubim, creatures that will dazzle your eyes to look upon. There, also, you shall meet with thousands and ten thousands that have gone before us to that place; none of them hurtful, but loving and holy; every one walking in the sight of God, and standing in His presence with acceptance for ever. In a word, there we shall see the elders with their golden crowns; there we shall see holy virgins with their golden harps; there we shall see men that by the world were cut in pieces, burnt in flames, eaten of beasts, drowned in the seas, for the love they bore to the Lord of the place; all well, and clothed with immortality as with a garment."
>
> Then said Pliable, "The hearing of this is enough to ravish one's heart. But are these things to be enjoyed? How shall we get to be sharers hereof?"
>
> Then said Christian, "The Lord, the Governor of the country, hath recorded *that* in this book; the substance of which is, if we be truly willing to have it, He will bestow it upon us freely."
>
> Then said Pliable, "Well, my good companion, glad am I to hear of these things. Come on, let us mend our pace."

WHAT DOES THE EARTH TEACH? 2

Speak to the earth, and it shall teach thee.

JOB 12:8

God has provided two great books for man's instruction—the book of revelation and the book of creation. The one is that volume whose name is familiar to us all—the Bible; the other is that wonderfully framed universe, whose silent pages are ever lying open to an observant eye.

The lessons of the book of revelation are known to a comparatively small portion of mankind. There are many millions of men and women who never heard of a Bible, and are utterly ignorant of its saving truths.

The lessons of the book of creation are within reach of every human being. The most unlearned savage has a great teacher close at hand, though, as a rule, he knows it not.

To both of these great books one common remark applies. A man may live in the full light of them, and yet be no wiser for them. The book of Scripture may be possessed, and yet confer no benefit on the possessor. To understand the Bible rightly, we need the teaching of the Holy Ghost. The book of creation may be open on every side of us, and yet we may see nothing of God in it. It is preëminently a volume which is instructive to none but an enlightened eye. "But he that is spiritual discerneth all things." (1 Cor. 2:15.) Once let a man's mind be guided by the Spirit of God, and he will see in both volumes things that he never dreamed of before. The Bible will make him wise unto salvation through faith which is in Christ Jesus. Creation, read with a spiritual eye, will confirm the lessons of the Bible. The words of God's mouth, and the works of God's hand, will be found to throw mutual light on one another.

Harvest is a season of the year which always draws me into this train of thought. Harvest, with all its interesting accompaniments, has a voice which always goes to my heart. I think of the thousands of strong arms which are clearing their way, over fields of wheat, and barley, and oats, from one end of the land to the other. I think of the thousands of eyes which are reading every square yard of our English cornfields. I think it useful, at a season like this, to remind people of the many lessons which the earth is continually teaching. I should like to sound in the ears of every farmer, and labourer, and gleaner in the land the striking words of Job—"Speak to the earth, and it shall teach thee."

But what are the special lessons which the earth teaches? They are many and various—far more than most people suppose—more even, I believe, than many true Christians ever consider. I am one of those who hold firmly that there is a close harmony between nature and revelation. Let me give a few examples of what I mean:

1. I believe, for one thing, that the earth teaches *the wisdom and power of God.*

This is a point which requires very little proof. None but an atheist, I think, would attempt to deny it. That the globe in which we live and move must have had a beginning; that matchless wisdom and design appear in every part of the framework of creation; that the minutest plants and animals, when viewed under a microscope, proclaim loudly "the hand that made us is Divine"[1]—all these are great first principles, which few will attempt to dispute. The denial of them involves far greater difficulties than the acceptance. No wonder that St. Paul declares: "The invisible things of Him from the creation of the world are clearly seen, being understood by the things that are made, even His eternal power and Godhead; so that they are without excuse." (Rom. 1:20.)

[1] Joseph Addison (1672–1719), *Ode.*

2. I believe, for another thing, that the earth teaches *the doctrine of the fall of man.*

How, I should like to know, can we account for the many enemies which often attack the best products of the earth, and prevent them coming to perfection? The weeds which impede the growth of corn, and require to be rooted up; the insects and vermin which prey on it—the slug, the caterpillar, the wireworm, and all their companions; the diseases to which the plant is liable, such as mildew, rust, and smut, and many others; from whence do these things come? They exist, as every farmer could tell us he finds to his cost. They interfere with the full development of many a harvest, and cause many a field to disappoint its owner of a full crop. But how can they be accounted for? I am bold to say that only one answer can be given to this question. That answer must be sought in the third chapter of Genesis, in the old familiar story of sin coming into the world. I assert confidently that nothing but the records of that chapter can explain the state of things which we see continually under our eyes. We cannot for a moment suppose that God created anything imperfect. Everything that God made was, like Him who made it, "perfect and very good" at the beginning. But something has evidently come in since the day of creation, which has defiled and marred God's handiwork. That something is sin! The earth, with all its beauty and fertility, is an earth which is still under the primeval curse—"Cursed is the ground for thy sake... Thorns also and thistles shall it bring forth to thee." (Gen. 3:17, 18.) I look for better days to come on the earth. I believe that the words of the psalmist shall be fulfilled when Christ returns the second time, and the curse is taken away. "Then shall the earth yield her increase," &c. (Ps. 67:6.) But in the meantime I believe firmly that the earth shows everywhere the footprints of sin.

The infidel and deist are fond of pointing to the works of nature, and bidding us look up through nature to nature's God. But let them explain, if they can, the anomalies and imperfections which no student of nature can fail to observe on the earth. I tell them boldly that they never can be explained without the Bible. The Bible alone can solve the problem. The Bible alone can make things plain. Without the Bible there are a thousand things in nature which would perplex and puzzle us. But when I read what happened in the garden of Eden, I see a solution of all my difficulties. I find that nature confirms revelation.

3. I believe, for another thing, that the earth teaches *the great truth that life comes out of death*.

No man, I imagine, can study what goes on yearly on the face of the soil without seeing that the death of one thing is the life of another. The annual death and decay of millions of leaves and plants is a part of the process by which vegetation is continually maintained. Leaf after leaf perishes, and contributes to the fertility and productiveness of coming years. Plant after plant is turned into rich mould, and helps forward the growth of another season. Even the seed corn which is sown exemplifies the same great principle. Grain after grain must die before there can appear "the blade, the ear, and the full corn in the ear."[1] The golden harvest which is reaped every autumn could never exist unless this great principle was annually worked out—that life springs out of death.

Now what is all this but a confirmation of one of the mightiest truths of Scripture? What have we here but light thrown on the great foundation of Christianity—Christ's death the life of the world? Hear what our Lord Himself says: "Verily, verily, I say unto you, Except a corn of wheat fall into the ground and die, it abideth alone: but if it die, it bringeth forth much fruit." (John 12:24.) The sacrificial death of Christ as our substitute on the cross is the foundation stone of the whole gospel. From His cross and grave spring all the lessons of a Christian. Take away His atoning death, and you take

[1] Mark 4:28.

away everything worth contending for in revealed religion. His death is our title to life; His sufferings the ground of our claims to glory; His crucifixion our warrant for expecting a crown. What intelligent Bible reader does not know that these are among the first principles of our faith? Is it nothing, then, that this great truth is pictured out every year on the face of the earth around us? To my mind, it is an unspeakable comfort. It helps, and strengthens, and confirms my faith.

4. I believe, for another thing, that the earth teaches the deep truth that *God acts as a sovereign in giving life where He wills.*

The profusion of vegetable life which the earth puts forth every year is so great as to baffle all calculation. Millions and millions of living seeds are called into existence which might, for anything we can see, become the productive parents of future vegetation. Yet millions and millions are never used for this purpose. Some are picked up by birds and insects, and used as food. Some fall into the ground and rot, and pass away. Even in the most carefully prepared cornfield, the proportion of seed corn that springs up and yields a harvest is far smaller than most people would suppose.

Now, why is all this? We cannot tell. The wisest course is to confess our ignorance. The facts are before us, and we cannot deny them. But how to explain the enormous annual waste of life which is incessantly going on is a problem that baffles man's understanding.

But does not this state of things assist us in considering that deep and mysterious truth, the sovereignty of God in saving sinners? We know that there are nations on the earth at this moment to whom God has never been pleased to send the light of the gospel. We know that there are thousands in our own land who, living in the full sunshine of religious privileges, remain dead in sin, and utterly careless about their souls. Graceless and godless they live, and graceless and godless they seem to die.

Now, if we attempt to explain this condition of things, we are brought to a standstill at once. It is a high thing, and we cannot understand it. It is a deep thing, and we have no line to fathom it. We can only fall back on our own ignorance, and rest satisfied that what we know not now we shall know hereafter. They that are lost at last will be found lost through their own sins and folly. The Judge of all the earth will certainly do right.

Yet surely the face of the earth around us may help us in considering the subject. The great fact that meets our eyes on every side, that not every living seed is allowed to live and grow up into a plant, is a fact that should be pondered well, and kept continually upon our minds. Whatever men may please to say about the doctrine of election in theology, they cannot deny its existence in vegetation.

5. I believe, for another thing, that the earth teaches us *the importance of a diligent use of means.*

The things that grow upon the earth contain in themselves a boundless capability of improvement. The gardener and the farmer know this perfectly well. It is one of the first principles of their business. They cannot give life. They cannot command success. "The earth bringing forth fruit of herself."[1] But when life has once been given, it seems to admit of indefinite strengthening and increase. By breaking up the earth and manuring it, by weeding and watering, by cleansing and protecting, by draining and irrigating, the results that may be produced are without end.

There is a spiritual lesson here, which is clear, plain, and unmistakable. Life is a thing that no man can give to his own soul, nor to the soul of another. But when life has once been imparted by the Spirit of God, there is no limit to the results  that may be produced by spiritual diligence and by pains in the use of means.

[1] Mark 4:28.

He knows but little who fancies that once converted he may sit still, and dream lazily along his journey to heaven. Let him know that his soul's prosperity is most intimately bound up with his soul's carefulness and labour. Let him resist the spirit of slumber, and work hard in the ways that God has appointed. Let him take heed to his Bible-reading and his praying, to his sermon-hearing and use of the Lord's Supper. Let him watch daily over his temper and his tongue, his company and his employment of time. Let him strive and agonise after a complete victory over the world, the flesh, and the devil. Let him remember that if it is worthwhile to do anything for his soul, it is worthwhile to do it well.

Well would it be for the Church if these simple lessons were more constantly kept in mind. Happy is that Christian who cultivates his soul as if it were a farm or a garden, and learns the wisdom of spiritual diligence from man's treatment of the land.

6. I believe, lastly, that the earth teaches *that great truth, the resurrection of the body.*

Nothing, perhaps, is more remarkable than the wide difference between the appearance of earth at the beginning of winter and at the beginning of spring. Thousands of herbaceous flowers in winter are dead down to the very ground. Not a vestige of life remains about them. The great majority of trees are naked and bare. The little child is ready to think they are dead, and will never put forth leaves again. And yet both flowers and trees are alive, and in due time will be clothed again with bloom and beauty. As soon as the warm air of spring begins to be felt, a resurrection takes place. To use the beautiful words of the Canticles—

> For, lo, the winter is past,
> The rain is over and gone;
> The flowers appear on the earth.
>
> (2:11, 12)

Cold must that mind be, and dull that heart, which does not see, in this great annual change, a lively type of the resurrection of man's body. He who formed the world foresaw the weakness of man's faith. He foreknew our slowness to believe spiritual things. He has taken care to provide us with an annual remembrancer of what He intends to do for our bodies at the last day. As plants and trees put forth life in spring, so in due time "our bodies shall rise again."[1] Well may we say, when we look at the difference of the earth in winter and in summer, "Why should it be thought a thing incredible that God should raise the dead?"[2] When sneering scoffers ask the question, "How are the dead raised up, and with what body do they come?" we may boldly reply, "Who art thou that talkest of difficulties? Speak to the earth, and it shall teach thee." "Thou fool, that which thou sowest is not quickened, except it die: and that which thou sowest, thou sowest not that body that shall be, but bare grain, it may chance of wheat, or of some other grain: but God giveth it a body as it hath pleased Him, and to every seed his own body. . . . So also is the resurrection of the dead." (1 Cor. 15:36–42.)

[1] Book of Common Prayer. [2] Acts 26:8.

3

DO WHAT YOU CAN

She hath done what she could.

MARK 14:8

THE text which heads this paper deserves attentive consideration. It contains words which were spoken by the Lord Jesus Christ in praise of a woman. Her name we are not told: this single action is all that we know about her. But she was praised by Christ. Blessed indeed are those whom the Lord commendeth!

The circumstances of the history are few and simple. Our Lord was sitting in the house of Simon the leper, at Bethany, "two days" before His crucifixion. The end of His work was drawing near; and He knew it. The cross and the grave were in sight; and He saw them. "As He sat at meat, there came a woman having an alabaster box of ointment of spikenard very precious; and she brake the box, and poured it on His head. And there were some that had indignation within themselves." They found fault with the woman's action. They said it was "waste." They murmured against her. But here at once the Great Head of the Church interposed. He declared that the woman had "done a good work." She had seized the last occasion she had of doing honour to her Master. She had used the only means she had of testifying her affection. And then He placed on her conduct the seal of His approbation in these solemn words—"She hath done what she could.... Wheresoever this gospel shall be preached throughout the whole world, this also that she hath done shall be spoken of for a memorial of her." Such was the occasion when these words were spoken. Now what are the lessons they are meant to teach us? There are two which appear to me to stand out prominently on the face of the sentence, two mighty principles which ought never to be forgotten. Let me try to show what they are.

I. We learn, for one thing, that the Lord Jesus likes His people to be *doing Christians*. He commends the action of the woman before Him. Others sat by in idle admiration, but never lifted a finger to do honour to their Messiah. It was very different with this woman. She "did" something. She did "what she could." Hence the praises bestowed on her. The Great Head of the Church likes *"doing"* Christians.

What do I mean by *"doing"* Christians? I mean Christians who show their Christianity in their lives—by deeds, by actions, by practice, by performance. True religion is not made up of general notions and abstract opinions—of certain views, and doctrines, and feelings, and sentiments. Useful as these things are, they are not everything. You must not rest content with them. You must see that they produce a certain line of conduct in daily life. The wheels of the machine must move. The clock must go as well as have a handsome case and face. It matters little what a man thinks, and feels, and wishes in religion, if he never gets further than thinking, and feeling, and wishing. The great question is, What fruit does the man bring forth? What does he do? How does he live?

"Doing" is the only satisfactory proof that a man is a living member of the Lord Jesus Christ, and that his faith is the faith of God's elect. True faith is not like the faith of devils, who "believe and tremble,"[1] but neither love nor obey. True faith will never be found alone, though it alone justifies. Where there is faith, there will always be love, and obedience, and an earnest desire to do God's will. Living members of Christ will always show something of their Master's mind. Weak as they may be, they love to follow His example whose whole life was action. It may be little that they are able to do, but that little they will try to do. We may be very sure there is no grace where there is no "doing."

[1] Jas. 2:19.

"Doing" is the only satisfactory proof that your Christianity is a real work of the Spirit. Talking and profession are cheap and easy things. They cost nothing. They are soon picked up, soon learned, soon forgotten, and soon laid aside. But "doing" requires trouble and self-denial. It looks like "business,"[1] and makes the world believe that religion is a reality. I care little to hear that a man likes sermons, and always goes to hear, and thinks sermons very good and very fine. I have lived long enough not to be satisfied with this. It is only blossoms; it is not fruit. I want to know what the man DOES. What does he do in private? What does he do in his family? What does he do on weekdays? Is his religion anything better than a Sunday coat—a thing put on every Sunday morning, and put off every Sunday night? If there is no "DOING" in a man's religion, it is not of the right sort. It has not got the true stamp on it. Like bad silver and gold, or plated articles, it has not got the Goldsmiths' Hall mark on it. It is worth little now; it will bring no peace on a deathbed; it will not pass the gate of heaven.

"Doing" is the only evidence that will avail a man in the day of judgment. Let any one note the conclusion of the 25th chapter of St. Matthew, and he will see what I mean. Your works will be the witnesses by which your faith will be tried. The question will not be, "What church did you attend? and what profession did you make? and what experience have you had? and what did you wish to be?" The only question will be, What FRUITS did your faith produce? "Faith," says James, "if it hath not works, is dead, being alone." (Jas. 2:17.)

Your works cannot justify you, my dear reader. They cannot save. They cannot put away our sin. Christ's work alone can do that. But there never was a justified man who did not do works—at any rate, some. Your works do not go before you into heaven, nor yet alongside of you. The souls that get there see none of their works. They only see Jesus Christ's

[1] Cp. Rom. 12:11 (AV).

precious blood and all-prevailing intercession. But your works are to *"follow"* you, if you are to go to heaven, in order to speak to your character. "Blessed are the dead which die in the Lord . . . that they may rest from their labours; and their works do follow them." (Rev. 14:13.) Never was there a greater mistake than to suppose that works are of no consequence because they cannot justify and cannot save. The supposition shows gross ignorance, and is a sad perversion of Scripture.

Are true Christians *God's workmanship*—are they new creatures? Yes! The Spirit made them what they are. But mark what St. Paul tells the Ephesians: "We are His workmanship, created in Christ Jesus unto good works, which God hath before ordained that we should walk in them." (Eph. 2:10.)

Are true Christians a *peculiar people?* Yes! God has chosen them out of the world, and called them to be His. But wherefore? St. Paul tells Titus that they may be "zealous of good works. . . . careful to maintain good works." (Titus 2:14; 3:8.)

Remember this dear reader. Let no man deceive you with vain words. Let none persuade you that "doing" is not an important part of Christianity. It is an old saying, "Handsome is that handsome does."[1] I will mend it. I say, "Christian is that Christian does." Would you be a happy Christian, and enjoy great comfort? would you be useful and a benefit to others? I trust many would like this. Then store up my advice today. Be a doing Christian. "Be doers of the word, and not hearers only." (Jas. 1:22.)

II. We learn, for another thing, from this woman's history, that *all true Christians can do something,* and that all should do what they can. What do I mean by "doing something"? I mean doing something for God's glory—something for Christ's cause—something for the souls of others—something to spread true religion—something to oppose the march of sin

[1] Oliver Goldsmith (*c.* 1728–1774), *The Vicar of Wakefield.*

and the devil—something to enlighten the darkness around us—something to improve and amend the world. Something or other, I say, every true Christian can do, and what he can do he ought to do.

Now I know well the devil labours to make true Christians do nothing. Doing Christians are the devil's greatest enemies. Doing Christians pull down his work, and weaken his hands. He will try hard to prevent your being a man of this character. I warn every one who has reason to hope that he IS a true Christian to remember this, and to be on his guard. Listen not to the reasons which Satan puts into your heads. Satan was a liar from the beginning, and you must not let his lies prevent you doing good. Stand on your guard, and be not deceived.

Satan will tell some that they are *too young* to do anything. Believe him not: that is a lie. The greatest men in the world and Church began to work, and were great, at a very early age. Alexander the Great conquered the world before he was thirty. Pitt was prime minister of England before twenty-five. It is never too soon to begin working for Christ. Yet a little while, and the enemy will say, "You are too old, and it is too late."

Satan will tell others that they *stand alone* too much to do any good. Believe him not: that is another lie. There never was a change for good or evil in the world's history which may not be traced up to one man. Martin Luther, Mahomet, Napoleon—all are cases in point. They all rose from the ranks. They stood alone at first. They owed nothing to position or patronage. Yet see what they did! Away with the idea that numbers alone have power! It is minorities, and not majorities, that shake the world. Think of the little flock Christ left behind Him. Think of 120 believers in the upper chamber of Jerusalem, and remember what they did to the nations. And then learn what wonderful things a few resolute hearts can do.

Satan will tell others that they have no *power* to do anything. He will say, "You have no gifts, no talents, no influence. You had better sit still." Believe him not: this also is a lie. Everybody has a certain degree of influence and weight on earth. Some have a ton weight, some a hundredweight, some a pound, some an ounce, some only a grain; but all have some. Everybody is continually helping forward the cause of God or the cause of the devil. Every morning you rise from your bed you go forth to gather with Christ or to scatter. Every night you lie down in that bed you have either been building the walls of Zion or helping to pull them down. There are but two parties and two sides in the world—the side of God and the side of the devil—the side of good and the side of evil. No man, woman, or child can ever be neutral, and live to themselves: one of the two sides they are always helping, whether they will or no. Grant that your gifts and powers are but a grain of sand; will you not throw that grain into the scale of God's cause? It is the last grain that turns the scale, and the last pound that breaks the horse's back. Grant that you have only one talent; see to it that your one talent is laid out as heartily for God as if you had a hundred. Ah, reader! it is not gifts that are necessary for doing good, but *will*. It is often the "one talent"[1] people that are the most slow to move.

But Satan will tell some that they have *no opportunities* for doing anything—no door open on any side. Once more I say, Believe him not: this also is a great lie. Never believe that you have no opportunity of doing good, till you are cast on a desert island, and cut off from the face of mankind; never till you are the last man in the world, never till then, believe that there is no opening for doing good.

Do you ask me what you can do? I reply, There is something for every true Christian in England to do. The least and lowest, the weakest and feeblest child of God is surrounded by people to whom he may do good. Have you not got relatives and connections, husband or wife, parents or children,

[1] Matt. 25:24.

brothers or sisters? Have you not got friends, or companions, or fellow servants? Have you not got masters, or mistresses, or labourers, or servants? Who in the world, almost, could say, No! to this question? Who but must say, Yes! If you say, Yes! then behold your opportunities of doing good. Harm or good you must do to all about you: you cannot help it. See to it that you do GOOD.

Have you not got a *tongue* to speak with? Might you not often speak a word of counsel? Might you not encourage the wavering, quicken the slothful, recall the backslider, check the profligate, reprove the worldly, advise the weak? Might you not often put in a word for God and Christ, and show your colours? Who can tell the power of "a word spoken in season"?[1] It has often been the salvation of a soul.

Have you not the power of doing good by *your life*? You may work wonders by steady consistency and patient continuance in well-doing. You may make people think by exercising graces before them, when they stop their ears against good counsel, and cannot be reclaimed by the tongue. Patience and meekness, brotherly kindness and charity, a forbearing and forgiving spirit, a gentle, unselfish, and considerate temper—all these have often a mighty effect in the long run. Like the constant dropping of water, they can wear away prejudices. Thousands can understand them, who cannot understand doctrine. There is such a thing as "winning without the word." (1 Pet. 3:1.)

I speak of things within the reach of all who have the will to do something for God. I might say more. The field is wide, the harvest great, and the labourers few. I might speak of the good that might be done everywhere by trying to teach the ignorant; to evangelize the wicked; to promote temperance, soberness, and chastity; to encourage honesty, economy, good temper, faithfulness, diligence, and sabbath-keeping. I might speak of help that might be given to charitable and religious

[1] Isa. 50:4.

societies, merely by making them known. Thousands of pounds might be got for home and abroad, if only men who cannot give themselves would ask others to give.

But I forbear. I have said enough to give food for thinking. Let a man once have the will to do good, and he will soon find the way. He will find that good can be done.

A true Christian should desire to leave the world, when he dies, a better world than it was when he was born, and should give his mite to improve it, whether in money, talents, or time. Let every man on earth who hopes he is a true Christian remember this. Let every one wake up, rub his eyes, look round him, and see if he cannot do something. Let no one say I can do nothing, unless he has tried. Let no one say he has tried, and it is no use, because he has not done everything that he wanted. There is much pride and mortified vanity in that thought. If we will do nothing unless we can do it perfectly, we shall do nothing at all. Let no one fancy he is doing no good, because he sees no immediate fruit from it. God's time is often not our time. Duties are ours and results are God's. But something let every true man of God try to do.

Set the Lord Jesus Christ before you, reader: and go forward in His footsteps, looking unto Him. Let Him be your strength, and let Him be your example. "He went about doing good."[1] Go and do like Him. You may be able to do very little: but DO WHAT YOU CAN.

[1] Acts 10:38.

4

WORDS FOR WOMEN

I HAVE often wondered what Bible-readers think of one particular chapter in the New Testament. That chapter is the last chapter of the Epistle of St. Paul to the Romans. What do they do with it? What do they get from it? What honey do they extract from its contents?

The last chapter of Romans is singularly full of names. The first fifteen verses are almost entirely taken up with greetings to persons of whom we know little or nothing. Many, I fear, are tempted to pass over them with a hasty glance, like the advertisement sheet of a newspaper, and to class them with the first chapter of Chronicles. "This is a barren land," they say to themselves; "there is little or nothing to be learned here."

Now, I believe that this way of viewing the last chapter of Romans is a great mistake. I believe that all Scripture is given by inspiration of God, and that every chapter is useful and profitable. I am one of those old-fashioned people who firmly hold that everything in the Bible is inspired. I have faith to believe that the hand of God is in the catalogues of Chronicles as well as in Romans 8, or John 14, 15, 16, 17. Believing this, I feel no doubt that there is a great lesson in Romans 16, and I will try to show what it is.

The chapter I have mentioned appears to me to contain a *special lesson for women.* The important position that women occupy in the Church of Christ—the wide field of real, though unobtrusive, usefulness that lies before them, if they will enter on it—the good service that they can do for Christ, if they have a mind—all these things seem, to my eyes, to stand out in the chapter, as if written with a sunbeam. I will proceed to show what I mean.

Observe, for one thing, that out of twenty-eight persons whom St. Paul names in concluding this precious epistle, no less than eleven, if not twelve, are women.

Observe, for another thing, the manner in which St. Paul speaks of these women. He says of Phebe that she was "a servant of the Church" and "a succourer of himself." He says of Priscilla that she was his "helper in Christ Jesus"—of Mary, that she "bestowed much labour on him"—of Tryphena and Tryphosa, that they "laboured in the Lord"—and of Persis, that she "laboured much in the Lord."

Now, I say there is much in all this to make us think. St. Paul was an apostle—a man chosen and called by Christ Himself—a man eminently useful in his generation—a man who possessed extraordinary gifts and singular fitness for his work—a man who seemed able, if anyone ever was, to stand alone and do without the help of others; yet see how this great apostle openly declares his obligation to a few weak women! See how he is not ashamed to publish to the world that they had strengthened his hands and refreshed his spirit, and helped him forward in his work. Let every woman that reads this chapter mark these things, and inwardly digest them.

I will write plainly the thoughts that come across my mind, while I read of Phebe and her sisters in Romans 16. I think how wide is the field of usefulness which is open to professing Christian women: and I wish every Christian woman who may read this paper to lay it to heart.

I say, then, that every woman may be most useful, if her heart is inclined to it. Every woman may do much, if only she is determined, and, like the Jews in Nehemiah's time, has "a mind to work."[1]

I would not be mistaken in saying this. I am not speaking of public work. All cannot be district visitors. All cannot teach schools, and direct Bible classes. All have not the gifts of Mrs. Stevens and Mrs. Fry. All cannot write like Hannah More and

[1] Neh. 4:6.

Elizabeth Fry.[1] Let those who have time, and gifts, and a clear call, give themselves to such work. But I speak of usefulness that all women can attain to—mothers with large families, wives with home engagements, daughters who must consult their parents' wishes rather than their own: and it is of them I say that every woman can do much.

I cannot away with the common notion that great usefulness is for men only, and not for women. Some women, I fear, come into this notion only too readily. I am afraid there is in some minds a kind of proud slothfulness that assumes the name of *humility*, and keeps people idle. Against this false humility let us always be on our guard.

A consistent Christian woman brings God before the eyes of those around her all the week long, whether they like it or not. She is "an epistle"[2] that none can help reading.

It should never be forgotten that it is not preaching alone that moves and influences men. There is something to be done, as the Apostle Peter reminds us, "without the word" (1 Pet. 3:1); and none have the opportunity of doing good so much in this way as women. Humanly speaking, the salvation of a household often depends upon the women.

To bring men, for example, to attend the means of grace, and regularly hear the gospel, is one grand object that a true minister sets before him. Every minister who "does the work of an evangelist"[3] must know how difficult it is to get some people to attend. There are always obstacles raised and objections started. If the men come one month, they do not come the next. It reminds one of our Lord's expression, "compelling them to come in."[4] And what is the reason of this? Often, far too often, I firmly believe, the simple account is discouragement from wife or mother at home.

[1] Harriet Mason Stevens (1841–1948) founded a girls' school in Burma, where she and her husband were missionaries; Elizabeth Fry (1780–1845) worked to improve living conditions for English prisoners; Hannah More (1745–1833) was "one of the most brilliant female ornaments of Christian literature" (Philip Schaff), dedicated to reforming children's education.

[2] 2 Cor. 3:2. [3] 2 Tim. 4:5. [4] Luke 14:23.

If women ask me in what way they can be useful, I answer, unhesitatingly and decidedly, first and foremost, by encouraging religion at home. Show your father, or husband, or brother that you take a pleasure in seeing him attend to his soul. Let your manner and your words show him plainly that you want to help him forward, and not to keep him back. Let your household arrangements be so managed that he shall see you will make any sacrifice rather than keep him from the house of God.

The fire of good inclination often burns very faintly in the conscience of a hard-working man. Let his wife or mother see that she stir and feed it. Let her beware, lest she be a wet blanket to put it out. The road of religion is a rough and uphill journey. Let her strive to take up every stumbling block, so far as in her lies. The cup of self-denial is a bitter one to weary flesh and blood. Let her labour, as far as possible, to make it sweet.

But, after all, there are a hundred little ways in which a woman can be useful in her own home, of which time would not allow me to speak particularly. Much is to be done by kind tempers, by gentle words, by meekness, by patience, by unselfishness, by attention in little things, by considerateness about little peculiarities, by thoughtfulness about little wants, by bearing with infirmities, and by "not answering again."[1] All these things tell in the long run. These are the constant dropping which can wear away the stone, the daily returning habits which influence men's minds. Whatever women may fancy, men's character is exceedingly influenced by their homes. Tell me the general character of a man's home, and I generally know something of the man.

It is a true saying, and a sad one, "Cold homes make full public-houses." I firmly believe that disorder, unkindness, and ill-temper at home drive many a working man into bad company, and make him seek relief in drinking, or frivolous

[1] Titus 2:9.

amusements. I have sometimes gone into the homes of poor men late in the evening, and found everything in confusion just before the husband came in from work—children dirty, unfed, and crying—nothing ready, nothing comfortable, nothing in its place. In such a case, I cannot wonder if the husband turns out ill. I am persuaded the true account of many a poor sot I see is just this—"made a drunkard by his wife."

If a woman would be useful, let her strive to make her home a happy one. Whether she be mother, wife, or daughter, let her make this her aim: that all the members of the family shall say, "There is no place like home."[1]

Let her strive to make the evenings of the day pleasant. It is the time when most men are wearied and worn with the labour of the day. A wise woman will endeavour to have a stock of cheerfulness in reserve for that time. Ah! these may seem small things to some readers. But you have much to learn of human nature, if you do not know the difference it makes to a tired husband, father, or son, if he finds a cheerful, pleasant, smiling face at home.

If a woman would be useful, let her look well to her home duties. Whatever place she may fill in a family, let her resolve that by God's help, she will fill it well. I count it nothing for a woman to be active out of doors however good her work may be, if she does not, at the same time, glorify God at home. Home is a woman's peculiar sphere, and let home, therefore, have her first attention. She ought to endeavour to keep all the machinery of the family in perfect order. She must try to help, to counsel, to restrain, to direct, according as need may require. She ought to make her husband, or father, or son, or brother feel that all is going on well in his absence—a post for everyone, and everyone at his post. There are a hundred little things in every family which need daily attending to, and none can attend to them so well as women. Little as they are, they can harass and vex a man's mind; and if he can be freed

[1] John Howard Payne (1791–1852), "Home, Sweet Home."

from their burden by a woman's thoughtfulness, it is no little gain to the peaceful working of the family. The scratch of a pin may be a trifle, but it can keep an elephant awake. Paul mentions it as a special duty of a woman that she should "guide the house."[1] It is said of the excellent woman in Proverbs that the heart of her husband "doth safely trust her"[2]—he knows that all is going on well while his back is turned. It is a high character that is given of Sarah, when Abraham could reply at once to the inquiry, "Where is Sarah?"—"Behold, in the tent."[3]

If a woman would be useful at home, let her watch well her opportunities of doing good. If she would do good to the soul of husband, father, or brother, let her pray continually for the spirit of wisdom and discretion. Of all people, she ought to remember that there is "a time to be silent," as well as "a time to speak,"[4] and to know the one from the other. She must not appear to set herself up as a teacher of men. There is a foolish pride about a man that makes him kick at the idea of a woman showing him anything he ought to know; and a woman who would do good must never forget that. She must try to win, not to compel; she must endeavour to draw, not to drive. A wife would be acting very foolishly who began preaching the gospel to her husband when he came in tired, wet, and hungry, without allowing him to rest, to clean himself, or to get refreshed. A sister would find her advice little valued by her brother who thought it proper to give it before company. A mother would be most unwise who gave her sons a severe lecture on the sin of drunkenness at the very moment when they came home intoxicated. Abigail showed her wisdom in not speaking to Nabal while he was full of drink; she knew that her words would be wasted on him, and waited till the morning. The wife of Samson might have known she would lose her hold on her husband's affections by teasing and vexing him in the days of the marriage feast. Esther watched

[1] 1 Tim. 5:14. [2] Prov. 31:11. [3] Gen. 18:9. [4] Eccles. 3:7.

her opportunity for speaking to her husband; she waited for the door to be made open for presenting her petition, and so gained her end. The saying of Solomon should never be forgotten: "A word spoken in season, how good is it!"[1]

A woman who would be useful in her own home must be careful to encourage the smallest beginnings of religion in those about her. The first actings of grace are often exceedingly small, so small as to escape observation. The first growth of gracious inclinations in a soul is often very slow, very easily checked; and if checked, perhaps retarded for years. No man can tell the importance of cherishing the first movings and drawings of the heart towards God. It may be only a willingness to hear, or a readiness to join in prayer, or a different treatment of the Bible; and yet this may be the first step that will lead on at last to a close walk with God. Blessed are those women who lend a helping hand at such a turning point in a soul's history, and take up even the smallest stumbling-block out of its way! Coldness and want of sympathy often throw the enquiring soul back. Happy is the man who has any near him to say, like Leah and Rachel, "Whatsoever the Lord hath said unto thee, do."[2]

I bring these things forward as seeds of thought. I hope that all women who read them will consider and think them over. I want them to understand how much they can do, how much depends on them, and how great is their responsibility in the sight of God.

Of course it would be easy to add to this paper. I might speak of the vast field of usefulness which is open to women in the training of children. It is not too much to say that the first seven years of life depend entirely upon mothers and nurses. The first seven years contain the foundation of character for life. The first seven years of young England are in the hands of women!

I might speak of what women may do in the matter of vis-

[1] Prov. 15:23. [2] Gen. 31:16.

iting the poor and ministering to the sick. There are hundreds of cases continually arising in which a woman is a far more suitable visitor than a man. She need not put on a peculiar dress, or call herself by a Roman Catholic name. She has only to go about, in the spirit of her Saviour, with kindness on her lips, gentleness in her ways, and the Bible in her hands, and the good that she may do is quite incalculable. Happy, indeed, is that parish where there are Christian women who "go about doing good."[1] Happy is that minister who has such helpers!

I conclude this paper by asking any woman who is not convinced by what I say to take up the Bible and run her eye over the histories it contains. If she wants proof of the influence that women have in their hands, let her notice how women leave their marks at almost every step in God's Word. Their influence, I freely grant, has not always been for good. But influence they have had, and influence they will have, as long as the world stands.

Eve in the garden of Eden, the daughters of men before the Flood, Sarah, Rebecca, Leah, Rachel, Potiphar's wife, Miriam, Pharaoh's daughter, Jethro's daughter, Rahab, Jael, Deborah, Jephthah's daughter, Delilah, Ruth, Hannah, Abigail, Michal, Bathsheba, Jezebel, Athaliah, Jehoshabeath, Belshazzar's mother, Elisabeth, the Virgin Mary, Mary Magdalen, Martha and Mary, Sapphira, Dorcas, Lois, Eunice —who that reads the Bible is not familiar with these names? Who can forget how they come up at almost every turn, and have a place and a portion in almost every story? To say, in the face of these names, that women have no influence, and are of no importance, is simply absurd. Let them know that they have a mighty influence, and let them use it for good. What the oil is to the machinery, what the whetstone is to the scythe, what the fire is to the steam engine, what the stream is to the waterwheel, all this the woman may be to the man. Let her remember it, and strive daily to do good.

[1] Cp. Acts 10:38.

5 LESSONS FROM NERO'S HOUSEHOLD

LESSONS from Nero's household! How strange that sounds. The master of that household was a bad man, if ever there was one. Nero, the Emperor of Rome, was a very proverb for cruelty, profligacy, tyranny, and wickedness of every description.[1] Yet this is the man to whose household the Bible sends us for instruction!

Lessons from Nero's household! It seems almost incredible. In the households of Abraham, or Moses, or Samuel, or Daniel, or Sergius Paulus, or Gaius, or Stephanus—in such houses we might well expect there was something to be learned. But who would ever dream of lessons from the household of the worst emperor that ever ruled over Imperial Rome?

But what are these lessons? and where are they to be found? They are to be found at the end of one of St. Paul's epistles. They form almost the last words which the great Apostle of the Gentiles wrote to his beloved Philippian church when he was a prisoner at Rome. He had probably dipped his pen in the ink for the last time when he put down those simple words, "All the saints salute you, chiefly they that are of Cæsar's household." (Phil. 4:22.)

I frankly confess that I have long read that verse with deep interest. I am one of those old-fashioned people who believe that every word of Scripture is given by inspiration of God; and that every verse is full of instruction, if we had only eyes

[1] Emperor Nero (37–68) was a beast of iniquity. During his reign, he murdered his mother, brother, and two wives (kicking one to death while she was pregnant). He also initiated the first imperial persecution of the Church, resulting in vast multitudes of martyrs—men, women, and children—suffering unspeakably cruel deaths, all for Nero's amusement.

to see it. I see in the verse before us two weighty lessons, which I should like to impress on every reader's mind. Who these saints were we are not told. Their names, their rank, their history, their difficulties, their work, their lives, their deaths, all are completely hidden from our eyes; and we shall know nothing more till the last day. We only know that there were "saints" in Nero's "household," and that they were courteous saints. Out of these two facts we will draw two lessons.

I. We see then, for one thing, in Nero's household, the *almighty power of our Lord Jesus Christ.* He could enable people to be Christians even in Nero's palace. By the grace of the Holy Spirit, which He planted in their hearts, He could give them power to be "saints" in the most unfavourable position that mind can conceive. With the Lord Jesus nothing is impossible; nothing is too hard for Christ's grace.

There is something to my mind most important in this lesson. It ought to come home with power to all who live in great towns. It ought to ring in their ears like a trumpet every day they live. It is possible to be a saint in a great city!

Great cities and towns, as a general rule, are most unfavourable places to a man's soul. Those who live in London, Manchester, Liverpool, or Glasgow know that very well. The whirl of business in which everyone seems to move, the incessant hurry to be rich in which all seem to be rushing along, the intense struggle to "get on," which seems to be the absorbing thought in everybody's mind—all this seems to make religion nearly an impossibility. Let a believer walk through Cheapside, or the Strand, in an afternoon—let him mark the careworn faces that he will meet at every step—faces in which money, money—business, business—is so plain that you could almost fancy you saw it—and if he does not ask himself, "How can the soul thrive here?" I shall be much surprised.

Now, if this be true of towns in Christian countries, what must be said of towns in heathen lands? What can we imagine more trying to the soul than the position of a Christian at Rome?

A believer at Rome would have all those trials which are the portion of the household of faith in every age—the trials which you and I find it so hard to bear—an evil heart, an ensnaring world, and a busy devil.

But a believer at Rome would have trials over and above these, of which you and I, living in quiet England, by God's mercy, know nothing.

He would live in a city where he might expect persecution any day, and where the name of Christ was scarcely known, and if known despised.

He would live in a city where idolatry was the fashion, where the temples of false gods would meet his eye on every side, where the mere fact of not bowing down to dumb idols would be an unusual thing.

He would live in a city where the gospel standard of morality was utterly sneered at; where the excellence of truth, purity, meekness, and gentleness would be unknown.

And yet, in spite of all this, God had a people at Rome. Here, in the midst of the darkest superstition and idolatry—here, in the midst of immorality and profligacy, the grace of God was proved all-powerful. Even here there was a church which could value the longest epistle Paul ever wrote. Even here there were "saints in Nero's household."

Can any one of us imagine the difficulties of a Christian in Nero's household? I suspect not. I believe that in a Christian country like this, amidst all the insensible restraints and benefits of scriptural religion, we can scarcely have the faintest conception of a heathen emperor's household eighteen hundred years ago.

We should have seen justice, purity, and truth daily trodden under foot. We should have had around us hundreds who neither knew nor valued the Sixth and Seventh Commandments. Our eyes would have been saddened by fearful sights, and our ears tortured by vile and defiling words. And even if our souls escaped damage, our lives and liberty would have been in constant peril. We might have felt every morning when we rose from our beds, "There is but a step between me and death."[1] Yet even in a position like this the grace of God triumphed. By the grace of God there were saints even in Nero's household.

The grace of God can make a man a Christian anywhere, in any position, under any circumstances, however unfavourable those circumstances may seem to be; and not only make him, but keep him so too. It can give him power to follow the Lord alone, while all around him are following sin and the world. It did so for Daniel at Babylon, for Obadiah in Ahab's court, for Lot in the midst of Sodom and Gomorrah, and for the saints in Nero's household.

It can enable a man to serve God amidst a family of ungodly relations. It can call him out and make him a witness for Christ, while all his kindred are walking in the broad way. It did so for Jonathan, the son of Saul; for Abigail, the wife of Nabal; for Josiah, the son of Amon.

It can enable a man to serve God in the most dangerous professions. It can keep him unspotted, while all around him are defiled. It did so for Cornelius the centurion in the Roman army, and for Zenas the lawyer.

I know the thought that is in many hearts. I know you fancy your position in life prevents your being a decided Christian. You say to yourself, "Had I a different master, or a different dwelling, different fellow-servants, or different friends, a different position in life, or different children, then I would serve the Lord." I warn you against this delusion. I tell you, it is not change of condition that you want, but grace.

It is not learning, nor money, nor the favour of the rich, nor the company of the saints, nor plenty of privileges; it is none of these things that makes a Christian. It is the grace of God that is wanted, and nothing else. It is the work of God the Father, God the Son, and God the Holy Ghost in the soul.

When the Spirit comes into a man's heart, he will be a Chris-

[1] 1 Sam. 20:3.

tian, notwithstanding any disadvantages. I defy the world, the flesh, and the devil, to keep them back. He will follow Christ, glorify God, and be saved, in spite of them all.

Till the Spirit comes into a man's heart he will never be a Christian, however great his privileges. No! not though he be servant to a prophet: Gehazi served Elisha. No! not though he be companion to a man after God's own heart: Joab was always with David. No! not though he be an apostle and a friend of apostles: Demas went about with Paul, and Judas followed Christ. Without grace no man ever will serve the Lord.

It is grace, grace, nothing but grace, that makes a Christian. You that would be saved remember this. Let this be your first step, your starting point—Come to the Lord Jesus Christ and ask for grace.

After studying human nature for twenty-four years as a minister, I feel that I ought to know something of it. I believe that one grand reason why many never take up decided religion is a dread of the difficulties connected with it. You say to yourselves, "It is no use; I never can alter; I never can break off from my old ways; I never shall be saved." I charge you, and entreat you, not to give way to such notions. I tell you that the grace of God can do anything. With grace nothing is impossible.

I have learned never to despair of any one as long as he lives, and is within the reach of the gospel. I may see no change in many at present. I may die, and see little or nothing done. But still I will hope on. I shall hope to meet in glory, at Christ's appearing, many of those who now walk in the broad way. They may be far off, but grace can yet bring them in; they may seem hardened, but grace can make them tender as a weaned child.

I do not despair of hearing that the most careless have learned that "one thing is needful"[1]—the most formal, that baptism and church membership are useless unless a man

[1] Luke 10:42.

becomes a new creature—the most self-righteous, that other foundation but Jesus no man can lay—the most scoffing, to delight in nothing so much as prayer.

I cannot despair with this verse of Scripture before me. I read this little sentence. I remember what Rome was. I remember what Nero was, and yet I see what grace can do. So long as I live I must and will hope on.

II. We see, for another thing, in Nero's household, a *bright example of Christian courtesy*. Many as the trials of these saints must have been, countless as their daily vexations and distractions, they did not forget to think of others. They had large and sympathising hearts. They remembered their brethren and sisters at Philippi, though, perhaps, they had never seen them in the flesh. And so, when they heard that the great Apostle of the Gentiles was writing to the Philippian church, they took care to send a kind message: "All the saints salute you, chiefly they that are of Cæsar's household."

There is something to my mind inexpressibly beautiful in this little message. It gives me a most pleasant idea of the ways and manners of the early Christians. It shows me that there was nothing rough, and hard, and stern, and harsh, and austere about their Christianity. Oh, no! They were a feeling, warm-hearted, loving, genial, considerate people. They were not entirely taken up with themselves and their own duties, crosses, conflicts, and trials. They could think of others.

Courtesy and consideration for others are Christian graces which receive far less attention than they ought to have. All like to be remembered by others, even if it is only in the postscript of a letter. None like to be altogether forgotten. "Little attentions," as people call them, are anything but little in reality; and that man knows little of human nature who fancies they are of no importance. None are above being pleased by them, whatever they may profess to the contrary. Courtesy, and civility, and manners may doubtless be made too much of; but, for all that, they are not to be despised. They are everything with some, and they are something with all. The

Christians of the New Testament day did not despise them, neither should we.

I fear there is a fault among Christians in this matter. Some behave in such a manner that one might fancy they thought it a Christian duty to be rude. But they have utterly mistaken the spirit of the gospel when they act so; and I tell them so now.

There is no true religion in rudeness. A man who is led by the Spirit ought to be more courteous and polite than others. "What do I more than others?"[1] should be his question. Certainly not, "What do I less?" He will have within him the roots of all true courtesy—humility and charity. He will be lowly in his own eyes, willing to count every one better than himself, and more worthy of honour, attention, and respect. He will be ready to take the lowest place, if need be. He will not be always thinking of self, self's ways, self's desires, and self's wishes; his great aim will be to make others comfortable and happy. Selfishness and pride are the two chief enemies of courtesy, and they are feelings to which a real Christian should feel ashamed to give way. Reader, depend upon it, to be uncivil and uncourteous is no mark of grace. 

Do we seek for examples of courtesy and considerateness in the Bible? Let us study the conduct of Abraham, as recorded in Genesis 13. See how he gives Lot the choice of the land—"If thou wilt take the left hand, then I will go to the right; or if thou depart to the right hand, then I will go to the left." Lot was a much younger man than himself, and could have found no fault if he had been left to take what Abraham rejected. Lot had no promise of the land for his inheritance, and had received no special marks of God's favour. Yet Abraham treats Lot as the most deserving of the two, declares himself willing to make any sacrifice, and is ready to make any arrangements by which peace and good feeling may be kept up between them. And he lost nothing by it at last. God loves to honour practical charity and humility.

[1] Cp. Matt. 5:47.

Do we ask for another example of courtesy? Let us study the character of the Apostle Paul. Let us mark how he frequently sends kind messages to individuals in the epistles that he writes to the churches. Amidst the constant thought and attention which the care of churches demanded—with all the anxieties of doctrinal and practical questions coming daily upon him—troubled on one side by Corinthian immorality, on another by Galatian false teaching, on a third by Hebrew scruples—who, I say, would have expected an apostle to remember so many persons, and to have sent them so many kind messages as are recorded in the last chapter of the Epistle to the Romans? And he reaped his reward. No wonder that Christians loved him tenderly, when they saw such largeness and sympathy of heart. No wonder that a great writer has called him "the most finished gentleman" the world has ever seen—the most complete combination of charity and humility.

I wish, with all my heart, that this subject received more attention than it does from the churches of Christ in the present day. I wish that Christians thought more of "adorning their doctrine,"[1] and making their religion lovely, beautiful, and attractive in the eyes of men.

I fear, even now, that many will think this lesson from Nero's household a matter of small importance. I fear that some reader is saying in his heart, "What waste of space is this! How much better to speak to us about inspiration or justification—about election, or grace, or the millennium, or unfulfilled prophecy! Who knows not such things as these?" Reader, if this be your thought, I am sorry for you. I think you have much yet to learn.

I call nothing *little* in religion which may be practised every hour of the day. From morning to night there is always room for exercising Christian courtesy and consideration.

I call nothing *little* which tends to make religion more beau-

[1] Titus 2:10.

tiful in the eyes of the world. Little arrangements make all the difference in the appearance of a room; little adornments make all the difference in the looks of a bride; little attentions make all the difference in the comfort a master feels in a servant. I am very jealous for my Master's cause. Anything, anything, to make it more lovely before man!

Cease, I beseech you, to think these things matters of little importance. The practice of them costs little, but the value of them, in the long run, is very great. A kindness of manner and demeanour—a readiness to sympathise with others, to weep with them that weep, and rejoice with them that rejoice—a forwardness to offer assistance when it seems likely to be wanted—a kind message in time of trouble, or a kind inquiry in time of sickness—all these may seem very small matters, but they are not so small as you think. They are not forgotten. They tend to increase your influence; they help to open a door of usefulness; they make people more willing to hear what you have got to say for your Master's cause. When people see that you care for them, they are more disposed to care for you.

Reader, study to be courteous and considerate. Pray for grace to be so. No man is so by nature. Few children can shut a door behind them, without being desired, or say "if you please" unbidden, or "thank you" without being taught. By nature we are all for ourselves.

I leave the subject now to calm consideration. Circumstances, no doubt, make a difference. Early habits, peculiarity of temperament, a solitary life, forgetfulness of mind—all these are things that will have an influence. It seems more easy to some people to be courteous than it does to others. But that all professing Christians should aim at courtesy, I am fully persuaded. Well indeed would it be for the cause of Christ, if all Christians walked in the steps I have tried to trace in this paper, and were like the "saints in Nero's household."

6

BE CONTENT

I.

The words which head this paper are soon spoken, and often cost the speaker very little. Nothing is cheaper than good advice. Everybody fancies he can give his neighbour good counsel, and tell him exactly what he ought to do.

Yet to practise the lesson which heads this paper is very hard. To talk of contentment in the day of health and prosperity is easy enough; but to be content in the midst of poverty, sickness, trouble, disappointments, and losses is a state of mind to which very few can attain.

Let us turn to the Bible and see how it treats this great duty of contentment. Let us mark how the great Apostle of the Gentiles speaks when he would persuade the Hebrew Christians to be content. He backs up his injunction by a beautiful motive. He does not say, nakedly, "Be content"; he adds words which would ring in the ears of all who read his letter, and nerve their hearts for a struggle: "Be content," he says, "with such things as ye have: for He hath said, 'I will never leave thee, nor forsake thee.'"[1]

Reader, I see things in this golden sentence which, I venture to think, deserve special notice. Give me your attention for a few minutes, and we will try to find out what they are.

I. Let us first examine *the precept which St. Paul gives us*—"Be content with such things as ye have."

These words are very simple. A little child might easily understand them. They contain no high doctrine; they involve no deep metaphysical question; and yet, simple as they are,

[1] Heb. 13:5.

the duty which these words enjoin on us is one of the highest practical importance to all classes.

Contentment is one of the rarest graces. Like all precious things, it is most uncommon. The old Puritan divine, who wrote a book about it, did well to call his book *The Rare Jewel of Christian Contentment.*[1] An Athenian philosopher is said to have gone into the marketplace at midday with a lantern, in order to find out an honest man. I think he would have found it equally difficult to find one quite contented.

The fallen angels had heaven itself to dwell in, before they fell, and the immediate presence and favour of God; but they were not content. Adam and Eve had the garden of Eden to live in, with a free grant of everything in it excepting one tree; but they were not content. Ahab had his throne and kingdom; but, so long as Naboth's vineyard was not his, he was not content. Haman was the chief favourite of the Persian king; but, so long as Mordecai sat at the gate, he was not content.

It is just the same everywhere in the present day. Murmuring, dissatisfaction, discontent with what we have, meet us at every turn. To say, with Jacob, "I have enough,"[2] seems flatly contrary to the grain of human nature. To say, "I want more," seems the mother tongue of every child of Adam. Our little ones around our family hearths are daily illustrations of the truth of what I am saying. They learn to ask for "more" much sooner than they learn to be satisfied. They are far more ready to cry for what they want, than to say "thank you" when they have got it.

There are few readers of this very paper, I will venture to say, who do not want something or other different from what they have—something more or something less. What you have does not seem so good as what you have not. If you only

[1] Jeremiah Burroughs (1599–1646); this book is an excellent read and is currently published by The Banner of Truth Trust.

[2] Gen. 33:11.

had this or that thing granted, you fancy you would be quite happy.

Hear now with what power St. Paul's direction ought to come to all our consciences: "Be content," he says, "with such things as ye have," not with such things as ye once used to have—not with such things as ye hope to have—but with such things as ye have now. With such things, whatever they may be, we are to be content—with such a dwelling, such a position, such health, such income, such work, such circumstances as we have, we are to be content.

Reader, a spirit of this kind is the secret of a light heart and an easy mind. Few, I am afraid, have the least idea what a shortcut to happiness it is to be content.

To be content is to be *rich* and well off. He is the rich man who has no wants, and requires no more. I ask not what his income may be. A man may be rich in a cottage and poor in a palace.

To be content is to be *independent*. He is the independent man who hangs on no created things for comfort, and has God for his portion.

Such a man is the only one who is always happy. Nothing can come amiss or go wrong with such a man. Afflictions will not shake him, and sickness will not disturb his peace. He can gather grapes from thorns, and figs from thistles, for he can get good out of evil. Like Paul and Silas, he will sing in prison, with his feet fast in the stocks. Like Peter, he will sleep quietly in prospect of death, the very night before his execution. Like Job, he will bless the Lord, even when stripped of all his comforts.

Ah! reader, if you would be truly happy (who does not want this?) seek it where alone it can be found. Seek it not in money, seek it not in pleasure, nor in friends, nor in learning. Seek it in having a will in perfect harmony with the will of God. Seek it in studying to be content.

You may say, It is fine talking: how can we be always content in such a world? I answer that you need to cast away your pride, and know your deserts, in order to be thankful in any condition. If men really knew that they deserve nothing, and are debtors to God's mercy every day, they would soon cease to complain.

You may say, perhaps, that you have such crosses, and trials, and troubles, that it is impossible to be content. I answer that you would do well to remember your ignorance. Do *you* know best what is good for you, or does God? Are you wiser than He?

The things you want might ruin your soul. The things you have lost might have poisoned you. Remember, Rachel must needs have children, and she had them and died. Lot must needs live near Sodom, and all his goods were burned. Let these things sink down into your heart.

II. Let us, in the second place, examine *the ground on which St. Paul builds his precept*. That ground is one single text of Scripture.

It is striking to observe what a small foundation the apostle seems to lay down, when he bids us be content. He holds out no promise of earthly good things and temporal rewards. He simply quotes a verse of God's word. The Master hath spoken. "He hath said."

It is striking, beside this, to observe that the text he quotes was not originally addressed to the Hebrew Christians, but to Joshua; and yet St. Paul applies it to them. This shows that Bible promises are the common property of all believers. All have a right and title to them. All believers make one mystical body; and in hundreds of cases that which was spoken to one may be fairly used by all.

But the main point I want to impress on men's minds is this: that we ought to make the texts and promises of the Bible our refuge in time of trouble, and the fountain of our soul's comfort.

When St. Paul wanted to enforce a grace and recommend a duty, he quoted a text. When you and I would give a reason for our hope, or when we feel that we need strength and consolation, we must go to our Bibles, and try to find out suitable texts. The lawyer uses old cases and decisions when he pleads his cause. "Such a judge has said such a thing, and therefore," he argues, "it is a settled point." The soldier on the battlefield takes up certain positions, and does certain things; and if you ask him why, he will say, "I have such and such orders from my general, and I obey them."

The true Christian must always use his Bible in like manner. The Bible must be his book of reference, and precedents. The Bible must be to him his captain's orders. If anyone asks him why he thinks as he does, lives as he does, feels as he does, all he has need to reply is, "God has spoken to such an effect: I have my orders, and that is enough."

Reader, I know not whether I make the point clear, but it is one which, simple as it seems, is of great practical importance. I want you to see the place and office of the Bible, and the unspeakable importance of knowing it well, and being acquainted with its contents. I want you to arm yourself with texts and verses of the Bible fastened down in your memory, to read so as to remember, and to remember so as to use what you read.

You and I have trouble and sorrow before us: it needs no prophetic eye to see that. Sicknesses, deaths, partings, separations, disappointments, are sure to come. What is to sustain us in the days of darkness, which are many? Nothing so able to do it as texts out of the Bible.

You and I, in all probability, may lie for months on a bed of sickness. Heavy days and weary nights, an aching body and an enfeebled mind, may make life a burden. And what will support us? Nothing is likely to cheer and sustain us so much as verses out of the Bible.

You and I have death to look forward to. There will be friends to be left, home to be given up, the grave to be visited, an unknown world to be entered, and the last judgment after all. And what will sustain and comfort us when our last moments draw nigh? Nothing, I firmly believe, is so able to help our heart, in that solemn hour, as texts out of the Bible.

I want men to fill their minds with passages of Scripture while they are well and strong, that they may have sure help in the day of need. I want them to be diligent in studying their Bibles, and becoming familiar with their contents, in order that the grand old Book may stand by them and talk with them when all earthly friends fail.

II.

FROM the bottom of my heart I pity that man who never reads his Bible. I wonder whence he expects to draw his consolation by and by. I do implore him to change his plan, and to change it without delay. Cardinal Wolsey said on his deathbed, "If I had served my God half as well as I have served my king, he would not have left me in my trouble." I fear it will be said of many, one day, "If they had read their Bibles as diligently as they read their newspapers, they would not have been devoid of consolation when they needed it most."

The Bible applied to the heart by the Holy Ghost is the only magazine of consolation. Without it we have nothing to depend on; "our feet will slide in due time." (Deut. 32:35.) With it we are like those who stand on a rock. That man is ready for anything who has got a firm hold of God's promises.

Once more, then, I say to every reader, arm yourself with a thorough knowledge of God's Word. Read it, and be able to say, "I have hope, because it is thus and thus written. I am not afraid, because it is thus and thus written." Happy is that soul who can say with Job, "I have esteemed the words of His mouth more than my necessary food." (Job 23:12.)

Let us examine, in the last place, *the particular text St. Paul quotes* in enforcing the duty of contentment. He tells the Hebrews, "He hath said, 'I will never leave thee, nor forsake thee.'"

It matters little to what person in the Trinity we ascribe

these words, whether to Father, Son, or Holy Ghost. It all comes to the same in the end. They all are engaged to save man in the covenant of grace. Each of the three Persons says, as the other two, "I will never leave thee nor forsake thee."

There is great *sweetness* in this peculiar promise. It deserves close attention. God says to every man and woman, who is willing to commit his soul to the mercy that is in Christ, "I will never leave thee, and never forsake thee." "I," the eternal Father, the Mighty God, the King of kings, "will never leave thee." The English language fails to give the full meaning of the Greek. It implies "never—no, never—no, nor ever!"

Now, if I know anything of this world, it is a world of "leaving, forsaking, parting, separation, failure, and disappointment." Think how immense the comfort of finding something that will never leave nor fail.

Earthly good things leave us. Health, money, property, friendship, all make themselves wings and flee away. They are here today, and gone tomorrow. But God says, "I will never leave thee."

We leave one another. We grow up in families full of affections and tender feelings, and then we are all thoroughly scattered. One follows his calling or profession one way, and another in another. We go north, and south, and east, and west, and perhaps meet no more. We meet our nearest friends and relations, only at rare intervals, and then to part again. But God says, "I will never leave thee."

We are left by those we love. They die and diminish, and become fewer and fewer every year. The more lovely—like flowers—the more frail, and delicate, and short-lived, they seem to be. But God says, "I will never leave thee."

Separation is the universal law everywhere, except between Christ and His people. Death and failure stamp every other thing; but there is none in the love of God to believers.

The closest relation on earth—the marriage bond—has an end. To use the words of the Prayer Book service, it is only "till death us do part." But the relation between Christ and the sinner that trusts in Him never ends. It lives when the body dies. It lives when flesh and heart fail. Once begun, it never withers. It is only made brighter and stronger by the grave. "I am persuaded," says St. Paul, "that neither life, nor death, nor things present, nor things to come, nor height, nor depth, nor any other creature, shall be able to separate us from the love of God, which is in Christ Jesus our Lord." (Rom. 8:38, 39.)

But this is not all. There is a peculiar depth of wisdom in the words "I will never leave nor forsake." Observe, God does not say, "My people shall always have pleasant things; they shall always be fed in green pastures, and have no trials—or trials very short and few." He neither says so, nor does He appoint such a lot to His people. On the contrary, He sends them affliction and chastisement. He tries them by suffering. He purifies them by sorrow. He exercises their faith by disappointments. But still, in all these things, He promises, "I will never leave nor forsake."

Let every believer grasp these words, and store them up in his heart. Keep them ready, and have them fresh in your memory; you will want them one day. The Philistines will be upon you; the hand of sickness will lay you low; the King of Terror will draw near: the valley of the shadow of death will open up before your eyes. Then comes the hour when you will find nothing so comforting as a text like this—nothing so cheering as a realising sense of God's companionship.

Stick to that word *"never."* It is worth its weight in gold. Cling to it as a drowning man clings to a rope. Grasp it firmly, as a soldier attacked on all sides grasps his sword. God has said, and will stand to it, "I will never leave thee."

"Never!" Though your heart often faints, and you are sick of self, and your many failures and infirmities: even then the promise will not fail.

"Never!" Though the devil whispers, "I shall have you at last. Yet a little time and your faith will fail, and you will be mine." Even then God will keep His word.

"*Never!*" Though waves of trouble go over your head, and all hope seems taken away. Even then the Word of God will stand.

"*Never!*" When the cold chill of death is creeping over you, and friends can do no more, and you are starting on that journey from which there is no return. Even then Christ will not forsake you.

"*Never!*" When the day of judgment comes, and the books are opened, and the dead are rising from their graves, and eternity is beginning. Even then the promise will bear all your weight. Christ will not leave His hold on your soul.

Oh, believing reader, trust in the Lord forever, for He says, "I will never leave you." Lean back all your weight upon Him: do not be afraid. Glory in His promise. Rejoice in the strength of your consolation. You may say boldly, "The Lord is my helper, and I will not fear."[1]

I conclude this paper with three practical remarks. Consider them well, reader, and lay them to heart:

(1) Let me tell you *why there is so little contentment in the world*. The simple answer is because there is so little grace and true religion. Few know their own sin; few feel their desert; and so few are content with such things as they have. Humility, self-knowledge, a clear sight of our own utter vileness and corruption, these are the true roots of contentment.

(2) Let me show you, secondly, *what you should do*, if you would be content. You must know your own heart, seek God for your portion, take Christ for your Saviour, and use God's word for your daily food.

Contentment is not to be learned at the feet of Gamaliel, but at the feet of Jesus Christ. He who has God for his friend and heaven for his home can wait for his good things, and be content with little here below.

(3) Let me tell you, lastly, that *there is one thing with which we ought never to be content*. That thing is a little religion, a little

[1] Heb. 13:6.

faith, a little hope, and a little grace. Let us never sit down satisfied with a little of these things. On the contrary, let us seek them more and more.

When Alexander the Great visited the Greek philosopher Diogenes, he asked him if there was anything that he wanted and he could give him. He got this short answer: "I want nothing but that you should stand from between me and the sun." Let the spirit of that answer run through our religion. One thing there is which should never satisfy and content us, and that is, "anything that stands between our souls and Christ."

7 "CERTAINLY I WILL BE WITH THEE"

EXODUS 3:9–12

THE words which head this paper are well known to all Bible readers. They were spoken by God to Moses in the day when He appeared to him in the burning bush.

At the time when they were spoken, the children of Israel were suffering hard bondage in Egypt. They were slaves under the tyrannical dominion of Pharaoh, King of Egypt—oppressed, afflicted, and trampled in the dust. Yet the Lord God of Abraham, Isaac, and Jacob had not forgotten His people. At the time appointed, He summoned Moses in the wilderness of Horeb to go back to Egypt and deliver his brethren from captivity. "Behold," He said, "the cry of the children of Israel is come unto Me: and I have also seen the oppression wherewith the Egyptians oppress them. Come now therefore, and I will send thee unto Pharaoh, that thou mayest bring forth My people the children of Israel out of Egypt."

But Moses was a man of like passions with ourselves. He saw the immense difficulties of the work proposed to him, and his first thought was to flinch and draw back. Forty years before, he had been only too forward. He had thought to relieve his brethren by carnal weapons, and in his zeal had killed an Egyptian. At the end of forty years he is ready to go into the other extreme. Age has cooled down that fiery heart, and in solitary communion with God he has learned his own weakness, and distrusts himself. "Who am I," he cries, "that I should go unto Pharaoh, and that I should bring forth the children of Israel out of Egypt?" At once he is cheered by a gracious promise, which deserves to be written in letters of gold, and remembered by all God's people—"Certainly I will be with thee." That promise turned the scale.

Now there are three lessons contained in the passage,

which all who desire to be true Christians will do well to remember. Let me try in a few words to explain what these lessons are.

(1) We learn, first of all, *what weak instruments* God sometimes uses to carry on His work in the world.

The children of Israel had to be delivered from the land of Egypt—redeemed from the hand of Pharaoh, and brought into the land of Canaan. This was a mighty work; indeed, a work surrounded with such immense difficulties that to the eye of man it might well seem impossible. Six hundred thousand men, beside women and children, with all their goods and possessions, were to be led through a howling wilderness, and planted in a country full of enemies. These men were a company of weak and timid serfs, without arms or money, and ground down to the dust by two centuries of most oppressive slavery. They were held in subjection by the most powerful king in the world, with an army prepared at a moment's notice to put down any attempt at insurrection. Such was the work to be done. Now what were the means that God used to do it?

He chooses for an instrument an old Hebrew, eighty years of age, who was keeping sheep in the wilderness. He suddenly gives him his commission, as he is feeding his flock on Mount Horeb, and bids him go back to Egypt, to deliver Israel from Pharaoh.

He gives him no money, no army, no weapon of war; no, not so much as a servant to accompany him. Alone He sends him forth on this astounding errand. "Come now," He says to Moses, "and I will send thee unto Pharaoh, that thou mayest bring forth My people."

It almost takes away our breath to think on the apparent impossibility of the work laid upon Moses. To the eye of man it seems like folly and madness. One single shepherd pitted against Pharaoh and the armies of the Egyptians! The very idea of such an unequal conflict sounds ridiculous and absurd.

Yet this is God's way. He loves to carry out His purposes in this marvellous fashion. Look over the history of His dealings with the world in all times, and you can hardly fail to see many like things.

Mark what He did when the proud giant, Goliath, was to be slain, and Israel to be delivered from the Philistines. He sent forth young David, without arms or armour, a shepherd youth, with nothing but a sling and five stones in his hand. Yet before that youth the haughty giant fell, and in a single day the power of the Philistines was broken.

Mark what He did when the time arrived for planting Christianity in the midst of the heathen world. He sent forth from a despised corner of the earth twelve poor and unlearned Jews—fishermen, publicans, and men of like occupation. He bids them preach a religion which to the Jews was a stumbling block, and to the Greeks foolishness. And yet, before the preaching of these men idolatry fell to the ground and melted away.

Mark what He did when He began the Protestant Reformation three hundred years ago. He raised up a solitary German monk, without money, rank, or friends, and put it into his heart to denounce popish error, and teach scriptural truth. Alone, and without carnal weapons, that monk proved more than a match for pope, cardinals, bishops, and all the hierarchy of Rome. Armed with the sword of the Spirit, that monk defied the thunder of the Vatican, and lighted a candle which is burning even to the present day.

Now why does God carry on His work in this fashion? He does it to hide pride from man, and to prevent man glorying in his own strength. He makes it impossible for man to say, "Our own wisdom, and our own might have given us success." When the huge host of the Emperor Napoleon was stopped in its career of victory—not by earthquakes, thunder, and lightning, but by silent frost and snow—all Europe was obliged to confess it was God's hand. And when the world sees the weak things confounding the things that are mighty, the world is forced to acknowledge, "This is God's doing."[1] It is the glory of a good workman to show his skill by making excellent work with bad tools. Just so, it is the glory of God's wisdom and power that He employs weak instruments to perform great exploits. "Not by might, nor by power, but by My Spirit"[2] is God's eternal principle of doing. He puts the treasure of the gospel into earthly vessels, that the excellency of the power may be of God and not of man.

We must beware lest a sense of our own weakness become a positive snare to us, keeping us back from attempting anything for God. There is a false humility in some men, which is only another name for laziness and cowardice. "Who am I, that I should do anything?" is their constant cry, when the real truth is that they are idle and afraid. What though you are weak as water and feeble as a child? yet the Almighty God is on your side. What though you stand alone comparatively—few with you, many against you? yet the Lord Jesus has said, "I am with you always."[3] Then fear not, but arise and try what you can do. There is much to be done for your own soul, and much for the souls of others. Try in the name of Christ, and you may yet find that nothing is impossible. Try in dependence on Christ's help, and you shall find that He who sent Moses from Midian to Egypt is One who never changes. He says Himself, "My strength is made perfect in weakness."[4] The Apostle Paul said, "I can do all things through Christ that strengtheneth me."[5] In sending missionaries to the heathen world, in evangelising overgrown parishes at home, in gathering congregations, in building schools, in aggressive measures on drunkenness and immorality, in bold opposition to false doctrine, in steady maintenance of pure truth, in speaking to sinners privately, in public preaching in season and out of season—in all these things try on, try on, and hold not your hand. Look not to your own feeble force. Wait not for ever,

[1] Ps. 118:23. [2] Zech. 4:6.
[3] Matt. 28:20. [4] 2 Cor. 12:9. [5] Phil. 4:13.

counting up allies and numbering supporters. Look away to Jesus, and go forward in His might. "When I am weak," said a mighty man of God, "then am I strong."[1] Think of the plagues of Egypt. Frogs, and flies, and lice, and locusts were not too small and insignificant to bring the wealth of Egypt to nothing. Moses, the solitary shepherd of Midian, was not too weak to bring Israel out of the hand of Pharaoh and the house of bondage. And you, even you, weak as you are, by God's help, may do great things for God, if you will only try.

(2) We learn, in the second place, *what doubts and fears* even a good man may feel.

We cannot doubt that Moses was a good man, and had the grace of God in his heart. It is recorded of him by the Holy Ghost that forty years before this time,

> By faith . . . he . . . refused to be called the son of Pharaoh's daughter; choosing rather to suffer affliction with the people of God, than to enjoy the pleasures of sin for a season; esteeming the reproach of Christ greater riches than the treasures in Egypt: for he had respect unto the recompence of the reward.[2]

Yet see how this man of faith shrinks and draws back when God proposes that he shall go back to Egypt. Great was the honour laid on him! glorious were the prospects before him! mighty was the God speaking to him! but, behold, even then this man of God doubts! "Who am I," he cries, "that I should go?"

He thought of *himself*. Who was he that, at the age of eighty, he should go from keeping sheep in Midian to address the King of Egypt, and demand the freedom of his people? Who was he that he should undertake to manage a nation of three million serfs, and lead them forth from Egypt to Canaan? And as he thought of these things, he doubted.

He thought of *Pharaoh*. Was it likely that a proud, self-willed tyrant like him would listen to the demand of an old Israelitish shepherd? Would the ruler of majestic Thebes, and

[1] 2 Cor. 12:10. [2] Heb. 11:24–26.

the builder of enormous pyramids, pay the slightest attention to a sudden summons to give up all his slaves? He thought of these things, and he doubted.

He thought of his brethren the *children of Israel*. Was it probable that they would believe his mission, and trust him as their leader? Would they, after being mentally and bodily crushed down by centuries of captivity, suddenly arise and venture all on the hope of an unseen promised land? Once more, I say, Moses thought of these things, and he doubted.

Now can I excuse him for his doubts? I cannot for a moment. I believe that the simple fact that the God of Abraham, Isaac, and Jacob was speaking to him ought to have silenced every fear. The simple fact that with God nothing is impossible ought to have checked any feeling of hesitation. All I say is that a man may be a child of God and yet be tossed about with inward conflicts. A man may have the faith of God's elect, as Moses had, and yet be brought low occasionally by a spasmodic fit of unbelief. The doubting spirit of Moses is not an example to be followed, but a landmark to instruct us, and a beacon to show us what we must avoid.

I am sure the lesson is one of vast importance. I suspect that scores of Christians go mourning all their days because they are ignorant of their own inward nature, and know not what they must expect to find in their hearts. They are apt to fancy they have no grace, because they see in themselves much remaining wickedness; and to think they have no faith, because they feel within a root of unbelief. And then comes the devil, and bids them give up God's service altogether. "You will never be able to serve Christ," he whispers; "you had better go back to the world."

Now I ask all such Christians to look at the case of Moses, and to take comfort. I do not tell them that their doubts and fears are to be commended; but I do tell them that they must not make them give way to despair. Painful and annoying as they unquestionably are, they are an ailment by which the best of saints have often been troubled. Like a broken tooth, or a foot out of joint, they may make your journey toward heaven very uncomfortable; but they are no proof that God has forgotten you, or that you will die in the wilderness. They are an humbling evidence that you are yet in the body, and need Christ's mercy every day; but they are no sign that your heart is wrong in the sight of God. Nay, rather, I am bold to say that where there are no fears there is no grace; and where there are no doubts there is no faith. So long as the world, the flesh, and the devil are what they are, God's children must expect to feel inward warfare, as well as inward peace.

But what are you to do with these doubts and fears? You must expect to meet with them; but of course you must not encourage them. They are Canaanites that will dwell in the land; but they must not be tolerated, countenanced, nor spared. You must resist them manfully, and watch and pray against them every day. You must not be thrown into confusion, like a raw recruit, at the first sight of the enemy; but be always on the lookout for him, and always ready to fight. You must form a settled habit of contending with unbelief, as a foe that never dies; and the longer you keep up the habit, the easier will the path of duty appear. The first steps toward heaven are, undoubtedly, always the hardest. When Moses stood on Pisgah, at the end of forty years, and saw Canaan spreading out before him in all its glory and beauty, I daresay he wondered that he could ever have cried, "Who am I?" When you and I find ourselves in heaven at last, we shall marvel that we ever gave way to doubts and fears.

(3) We learn, lastly, *what kind of encouragement* God gives to doubting people. He answered the fears and questionings of Moses with one broad gracious promise—"Certainly I will be with thee." The wisdom and fulness of that sentence are alike admirable. The more we look at it—like the cloud which Elijah's servant saw rising from the sea—the greater and more satisfying shall we find it to be.

God did not promise Moses that he should have no cross

or trouble. He did not say that Pharaoh would prove gentle and kind, and at once grant everything that was wanted. He did not undertake that the path to Canaan would present no difficulties, and that Israel would be faithful and obedient throughout the journey. He simply declared, "I will be with thee." In every time, in every circumstance, in every place, in every company, in every condition, I will be at thy side.

It was a promise of *companionship*. When thou standest alone before Pharaoh and all his courtiers, despised, insulted, and scorned—when thou goest forth toward the Red Sea, not knowing how thy people are to cross over—when thou findest thy people faithless and idolatrous in the wilderness, and even Aaron timid and vacillating—even then thou shalt not be alone. I will be with thee!

It was a promise of *protection*. When the fierce Egyptian army pursues thee, and all hope of escape seems cut off—when Amalek, and Moab, and the Amorite oppose thee, and the way to Canaan seems barred—even then I will be thy shield and defender. I will be with thee!

It was a promise of *advice and counsel*. When thou standest by the shore of the Red Sea, not knowing what to do for the timid multitude around thee—when there seems neither bread to eat nor water to drink in the wilderness—when even thine own people murmur against thee, and are ready to cast off thine authority—even then I will not leave thee destitute of counsel. I will be with thee!

What a glorious promise was this! How admirably it suited the occasion! Well did that all-wise God who spoke it know the want and necessities of man's heart. Well did He know that nothing cheers and supports us in trial like companionship, that nothing so nerves and sustains us in the hour of darkness as the society of a strong friend. Over and over again I find the same promise given to God's children. It seems as if God had nothing better and nothing greater to bestow on them than His own company. When Jacob was ordered to go back to his father's country, the LORD said, "Return, and I will be with thee."[1] When Joshua was appointed leader of Israel, in place of Moses, the LORD said, "As I was with Moses, so I will be with thee."[2] When Paul was preaching the gospel almost alone at Corinth, the Lord said, "I am with thee, and no man shall set on thee to hurt thee."[3] When Jesus was about to leave His apostles alone in the world, the parting words of encouragement He spoke were simply these: "I am with you always, even unto the end of the world."[4]

What, after all, can a Christian desire better than the company of God and His Christ? Where He is, there must be safety. Where He is, His people can take no harm. What does an infant care for house, or rooms, or climate, or furniture, so long as it feels its loving mother's arm around it? And what can a Christian possibly lack that is for his good, so long as Jesus Christ is by his side? He may be called to go to the farthest corner of the earth; but he will not go alone. He may be placed in the most difficult post of duty; but he has near him a helper. He may have a heavy cross to bear; but he has by his side a friend. Live for the world, and sin, and pleasure, and you are sure one day to find yourself alone, helpless, friendless, desolate, none to comfort, and none to cheer. But live for God and for Christ, and you are never alone. You have always the best of companions. You are always guarded, kept, watched over, and cared for by love that passeth knowledge.

Reader, I leave the subject here: I only ask you, as we part, to remember that whatsoever things were written aforetime were written for our learning. That glorious promise, "Certainly I will be with thee," was not meant for Moses only, but for every true Christian. Lay hold on this promise, and go forward in God's name, and be bold in God's service. Lay hold on it, and be not afraid. None ever laid their weight on it and found it fail. Is it not written by Him that cannot lie, "Heaven and earth shall pass away, but My words shall not pass away"?[5]

[1] Gen. 31:3. [2] Josh. 1:5. [3] Acts 18:10.
[4] Matt. 28:20. [5] Matt. 24:35; Mark 13:31; Luke 21:33.

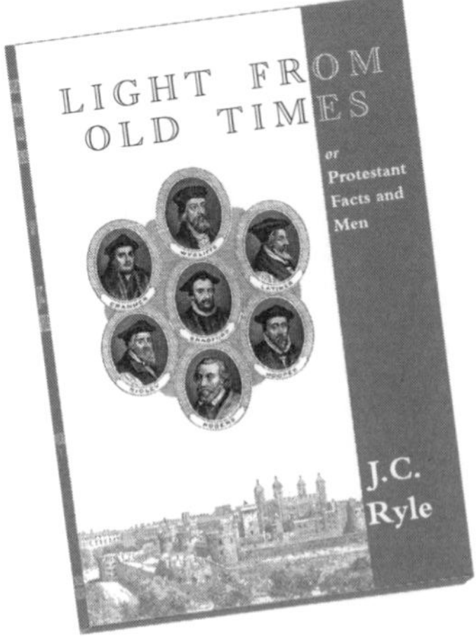

Beneath the sands of time lie the ashes of saints who were burnt alive for every single Protestant freedom we now enjoy. Written to our "children's children," these pages extol the faith—in life and in death—of the saints who delivered the English-speaking gospel to us. Vol. I of the collected works, 430 Smythe-sewn pages, ISBN 0-9677603-0-5.

Reformed, evangelical, and Protestant to the bone, *Knots* is considered by many to be Ryle's *magnum opus:* "Let us have clear systematic views of the gospel of the grace of God. Nothing else will do good in the hour of sickness, in the day of trial, on the bed of death, and in the swellings of Jordan." Vol. IV, 445 Smythe-sewn pages, ISBN 0-9677603-2-1.

www.charlesnolanpublishers.com

Few themes stirred Ryle more than the Bible, and this volume sets forth abundant reasons why all men—especially believers—should be stirred up as well. "It is still the first book which fits the child's mind when he begins to learn religion, and the last to which the old man clings as he leaves the world." Paperback, 68 pages, ISBN 0-9677603-3-X.

Searching, convicting, edifying, and ultimately God-honoring—*Holiness,* to borrow the apostle's words, is *"unspeakable and full of glory."* It is a life-changer. It is quite simply magnificent. And now it is completely unabridged. Vol. VII of the collected works, 440 Smythe-sewn pages, ISBN 0-9677603-4-8 (hc), 0-9677603-5-6 (pbck).

Shall We Know One Another?
&
Other Papers
by
J.C. Ryle

Set in 11.5 on 13.5 Adobe Jenson
on
60# Husky Offset
Composed at
Ruptüred Disc Studios
Printed & Bound by
Jostens Printing & Publishing

Line art from
"Principles of Light and Shade"
by
Leonardo da Vinci
Cover design by
CAROLUS MAGNUS